Chambers

FIRST PICTURE DICTIONARY

Chambers
FIRST PICTURE DICTIONARY

Betty Root MBE has been the Director of the Reading and Language Information Centre at the University of Reading since its establishment in 1968. She has lectured in the UK and overseas on many aspects of the teaching of reading.

Betty Root is well known as a writer, editor and reviewer of children's books. She has devised and published many reading games and written several dictionaries.

Rosemary McMullen has illustrated a number of children's books and designed many book covers. She has worked with Betty Root on several projects.

Chambers

FIRST PICTURE DICTIONARY

Betty Root

ILLUSTRATED BY
Rosemary McMullen

Published by W & R Chambers Ltd, Edinburgh, 1988

British Library Cataloguing in Publication Data

Root, Betty
    Chambers first picture dictionary
    1. English language—Dictionaries,
    juvenile
    I. Title. II. McMullen, Rosemary
    423   PE1628.5

    ISBN 0-550-10644-8

Colour separation by Creative Colour Repro, Glasgow.

Typeset by Image Services Ltd, Edinburgh

Printed in Great Britain by The Eagle Press PLC

INTRODUCTION

This colourful picture dictionary is suitable for children from five to nine years. The youngest children will enjoy recognising and naming the pictures and in doing so will learn to recognise the printed word. The older children will learn about definitions and spelling.

The words selected are those which young children frequently use in their early writing. This fact has been established by careful analysis of a number of children's home-made word books taken from different schools.

All the pictures have been checked with children of the appropriate age to avoid the possibility of ambiguity. The pictures therefore really do cue children into the written word.

Definitions have been written in simple language so that the actual task of reading does not interfere with getting the meaning from print.

Many published picture word books ignore these commonsense rules. Often the definitions are far too complicated for young children to read; the illustrations do not clearly indicate which words they represent; many of the words selected are not commonly used by children.

Chambers First Picture Dictionary is clear, uncluttered, beautifully illustrated and well researched.

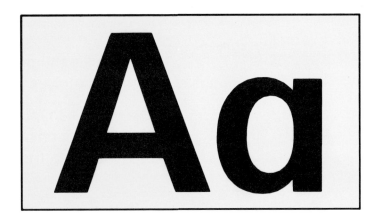

a b c d e f g h i j k l m n o p q r s t u v w x y z

acorn

An acorn is the seed of an oak tree. Acorns grow in little cups and squirrels like to eat them.

acrobat

An acrobat is a person in a circus who can do special tricks.

Some acrobats walk on a tight-rope high in the air.

Sam would like to be an acrobat in the circus when he is older.

add

$$+\frac{2}{3}$$
$$=5$$

To add means to put things like numbers together. When you add two and two the answer is four.

To add also means to put in.

If you make a cake you add eggs to the mixture.

a
b
c
d
e
f
g
h
i
j
k
l
m
n
o
p
q
r
s
t
u
v
w
x
y
z

aerial

An aerial is the part of a radio or television set that receives signals.

The workmen came and put a television aerial on our chimney so that we could see the picture on the screen.

aeroplane

An aeroplane is a machine that flies in the air. Aeroplanes get you to places very quickly because they can fly fast.

When you look out of an aeroplane window people on the ground look very small.

alligator

An alligator is a long animal with a thick skin. It lives in lakes and rivers in America and China. Alligators look like crocodiles.

a b c d e f g
h i j k l m n o
p q r s t u v w
x y z

alphabet

The alphabet is what we call all the letters we use for writing. There are twenty-six letters in the alphabet.

anchor

An anchor is a very heavy metal hook which is dropped to the bottom of the sea to stop a boat from moving.

The pirates dropped the anchor of their boat because they wanted to jump aboard another boat.

2

animal

An animal is any living thing that is not a plant. Not all animals have four legs; fishes and snakes are animals.

Many different animals live in the hot jungle and some of them are dangerous.

ankle

Your ankle is the part of your body between your leg and foot.

Footballers sometimes hurt their ankles when they fall.

apple

An apple is a round juicy fruit. Apples can be red or green.

All the apples on the trees in the orchard are ripe and ready to pick.

apron

An apron is something you wear over your clothes to keep them clean.

When my Mum cleans the oven she wears an apron because it is such a dirty job.

aquarium

An aquarium is a glass or plastic container in which you keep fish or other water animals.

My friend keeps tropical fish in an aquarium.

a
b
c
d
e
f
g
h
i
j
k
l
m
n
o
p
q
r
s
t
u
v
w
x
y
z

a
b
c
d
e
f
g
h
i
j
k
l
m
n
o
p
q
r
s
t
u
v
w
x
y
z

arm

Your arm is the part of your body between your shoulder and your hand. You have two arms, one on each side of your body.

arrow

An arrow is a thin stick which has a sharp point at one end and feathers at the other.

Long ago, soldiers used bows and arrows in battles.

An arrow is also a sign.

The arrow painted on the road showed which way to go.

astronaut

An astronaut is a person who flies in a spacecraft.

It was very exciting when an astronaut landed on the moon for the very first time.

athlete

An athlete is a person who is good at running or other sports.

Many athletes took part in the Olympic Games. They were all trying to win gold medals.

axe

An axe is a sharp metal tool with a wooden handle.

Chopping down a tree with an axe is very hard work.

Bb

baby

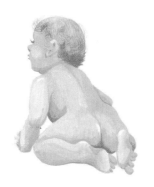

A baby is a very young child who has not yet learnt to walk. A baby can be a boy or a girl.

back

The back of a person is the part behind the chest. The back of an animal is the part on top of the body.

Back can also mean any part behind.

John went round the house to the back door.

badger

A badger is a black and white furry animal which is very shy.

When it was dark the badger came out of its hole in the ground to look for food.

bag

A bag is used to hold things. Bags can be made of paper, plastic or material.

a
b
c
d
e
f
g
h
i
j
k
l
m
n
o
p
q
r
s
t
u
v
w
x
y
z

bagpipes

Bagpipes are a musical instrument with pipes and a bag.

A soldier was standing near the castle playing the bagpipes.

baker

A baker is a person who bakes and sells bread and cakes.

My uncle is a baker and he made me a big cake for my birthday party.

ball

A ball is a round toy used in many games like football and tennis.

It is very difficult to catch a ball when you throw it high into the air.

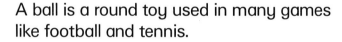

balloon

A balloon is a bag filled with air. Some balloons are small and you can play with them in the house.

Some balloons are very big indeed; these are called hot air balloons because the air inside them is hot.

banana

A banana is a long curved fruit which has a thick yellow skin on the outside and is soft and cream-coloured inside.

6

band

A band is a group of people who play music together.

bandage

A bandage is a piece of thin white material used to cover up a wound.

The nurse put a bandage round Jim's finger because he had cut it.

bank

A bank is a place where you put your money to keep it safe.

A bank is also the side of a river.

The fisherman sat down on the bank to do some fishing.

barrel

A barrel is a large round wooden container.

In the hotel there were lots of barrels full of beer.

basket

A basket is used to hold things and is made from strong material like wood or plastic.

I carry my shopping in a basket.

a
b
c
d
e
f
g
h
i
j
k
l
m
n
o
p
q
r
s
t
u
v
w
x
y
z

bat

A bat is a little animal which looks like a mouse with wings.

Bats fly mostly at night.

A bat is also a strong wooden stick used to hit a ball.

bath

A bath is a very large container which you fill with water and sit in so that you can wash all over.

bear

A bear is a large wild animal which has long fur.

This fur can be black, brown or white.

bed

A bed is a piece of furniture used to sleep or rest on.

Our naughty dog was sleeping on my bed instead of in his own basket.

bee

A bee is a flying insect with six legs and a sting.

It feeds on nectar and pollen in flowers and bees make honey from this.

It was a hot sunny day and the bees were flying in and out of the flowers in the garden.

beetle

A beetle is an insect with hard front wings. Some beetles damage plants.

bell

A bell is a hollow metal object which looks like a cup upside down. When you shake or hit a bell, it makes a ringing sound.

The village church bells ring on Sundays and after weddings.

bicycle

A bicycle is a machine with two wheels for riding on. When you push on the two pedals the wheels go round.

Some people take a long time to learn to ride a bicycle. They cannot balance and keep falling off.

binoculars

Binoculars are like two telescopes joined together. When you look through them things far away seem much closer.

Dad wanted to know what kind of bird was in the tree, so he looked through his binoculars.

biscuit

A biscuit is something you eat which has been made with flour, eggs and sugar, then cooked.

a
b
c
d
e
f
g
h
i
j
k
l
m
n
o
p
q
r
s
t
u
v
w
x
y
z

bite

To bite is to cut or hurt with your teeth.

If you are unkind to a dog it may bite you.

black

Black is a very dark colour.

blackberry

A blackberry is a sweet juicy fruit which grows on bushes.

In the Autumn we picked lots of blackberries and made them into jam.

blackboard

A blackboard is a piece of wood painted black. You can write on a blackboard with chalk; then you can rub it out.

bleed

To bleed is to lose blood.

My finger started to bleed when I cut it on a knife.

blow

To blow is to send air out of the mouth.

On his birthday Jack blows out the candles on his cake.

A blow is also a hard knock.

blue

Blue is the colour of the sky when there are no clouds in it.

Lots of flowers are blue. Can you name any of them?

boat

A boat is what you ride in when you travel on water.

Tom sailed over to the other side of the river in his boat.

bone

A bone is one of the hard white parts in your body underneath your skin. Animals have bones too.

When Mary fell off the swing she broke a bone in her arm.

book

A book is a number of pieces of paper fastened together. You usually find words and pictures in a book.

This dictionary is a book.

a
b
c
d
e
f
g
h
i
j
k
l
m
n
o
p
q
r
s
t
u
v
w
x
y
z

boot

A boot is a kind of heavy shoe which covers your feet and ankles.

The boot is also the space in the back of a car where you can put luggage.

bottle

A bottle is a container which holds liquids. It can be made of glass or plastic. You sometimes get milk in a bottle.

bow

A bow is a knot tied with two loops.

Carol tied the ribbon in a bow round her teddy bear's neck.

A bow is also a curved piece of wood with a tight string joining the two ends. You use a bow to shoot arrows.

box

A box is a container with straight sides. It can be made of wood, cardboard or plastic.

To box means to fight with your fists.

boxer

A boxer is a person who fights with his fists. Boxers wear big gloves to protect their hands.

bracelet

A bracelet is a chain or band which you wear on your wrist or arm.

When the baby was born she was given a little silver bracelet.

bread

Bread is a food which is made from flour, yeast, water and fat. People often eat butter and jam with bread.

breakfast

Breakfast is the first meal of the day.

Tom eats cornflakes for his breakfast before he goes to school. His Dad likes to have bacon and egg.

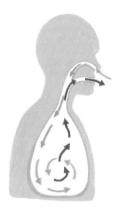

breathe

To breathe is to take air into your lungs and then push it out.

If you stop breathing for a long time you will die.

brick

A brick is a hard piece of earth which has been baked.

The big fat pig built his house with bricks to make it strong so that the wolf could not blow it down.

a b c d e f g h i j k l m n o p q r s t u v w x y z

bride

A bride is a woman on her wedding day.

bridegroom

A bridegroom is a man on his wedding day.

bridge

A bridge is something built over a river, road or railway so that you can get to the other side.

brown

Brown is the colour of chocolate or the earth.

Sue has brown hair and brown eyes.

brush

A brush is a bundle of hairs fixed to a handle. You use one kind of brush to sweep up rubbish and another to brush your hair.

bucket

A bucket is a container for carrying water. It has a handle and is made of metal or plastic.

Nick filled a bucket with water so that he could wash his car.

bud

A bud is a flower or a leaf before it opens.

In the Spring the trees are full of buds. When the weather gets warmer the buds turn into green leaves or flowers.

bulldozer

A bulldozer is a very big machine which can move huge piles of earth and stones.

When the men dug a big hole in the road the bulldozer pushed away all the earth.

burglar

A burglar is a person who breaks into a house or shop and steals things.

The policeman caught the burglar stealing jewels from a shop.

a
b
c
d
e
f
g
h
i
j
k
l
m
n
o
p
q
r
s
t
u
v
w
x
y
z

bus

A bus is a large car which can carry lots of people.

When you ride on a bus you have to buy a ticket.

butcher

A butcher is a person who cuts up meat and sells it.

Mum sent me to the butcher to buy some pork chops for dinner.

butterfly

A butterfly is an insect with very pretty coloured wings. Butterflies fly about in the daytime. They grow from caterpillars.

button

A button is a hard flat object which fastens clothes.

A button came off my coat so I had to sew it on again.

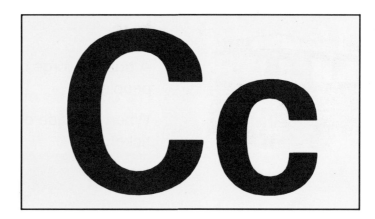

Cc

cactus

A cactus is a plant covered with prickles.

cage

A cage is like a big box with bars.

Some animals are kept in cages.

At the circus the lion was kept in a cage because he was too dangerous to wander about.

cake

A cake is a sweet food made from sugar, flour, eggs and butter.

People sometimes eat cake at teatime.

calculator

A calculator is a machine that can work out sums. You can do sums very quickly on a calculator.

a b c d e f g h i j k l m n o p q r s t u v w x y z

calf

A calf is a young cow.

The calf sucks milk from its mother.

camel

A camel is a large animal that lives in the desert. It has one or two humps on its back. You can ride on a camel or use it to carry heavy loads.

camera

You take photographs with a camera. It has a special piece of glass at the front called a lens.

canary

A canary is a small yellow bird. You can keep a canary as a pet in a cage.

Penny likes her canary because it sings every morning.

candle

A candle is a stick of wax. It has a string in the middle called a wick. Candles give light.

Lucy had 5 candles on her birthday cake. She blew them all out in one go.

canoe

A canoe is a small, narrow boat. You use paddles to make a canoe move through the water.

cap

A cap is a small hat. You wear a cap on your head.

Peter put his cap on before he went to school.

car

A car is a vehicle with four wheels and an engine. There are seats inside a car for the driver and passengers to sit on.

Going by car is much quicker than walking.

caravan

A caravan is a small house on wheels. Most caravans have to be pulled along behind a car. Some people go on holiday in a caravan.

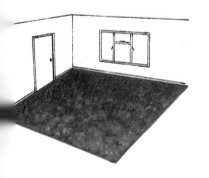

carpet

A carpet is something which covers the floor. It is usually made of wool or nylon.

Helen dropped the bottle of milk and it went all over the new carpet.

a
b
c
d
e
f
g
h
i
j
k
l
m
n
o
p
q
r
s
t
u
v
w
x
y
z

a
b
c
d
e
f
g
h
i
j
k
l
m
n
o
p
q
r
s
t
u
v
w
x
y
z

carrot

A carrot is a long, thin orange-coloured vegetable which grows in the ground. You can eat carrots raw or cooked.

carry

To carry is to pick up something and move it from one place to another.

Tom likes to carry the shopping-basket for his Mum.

carve

To carve is to cut meat into slices.

Dad uses a sharp knife to carve the joint of beef.

case

A case is a kind of box to put things in.

When Jim goes on holiday he takes his clothes in a case.

castle

A castle is a very large old building with thick stone walls. Castles were built very strong to keep out enemy soldiers.

The castle has a drawbridge.

cat

A cat is a furry animal with a long tail. Many people keep a cat for a pet.

Our cat loves to sleep in front of the fire where it is warm.

catch

To catch is to get hold of something or someone which is moving.

Bob is trying to catch the ball.

caterpillar

A caterpillar is an insect which looks like a furry worm. When the caterpillar grows it turns into a butterfly.

cauliflower

A cauliflower is a vegetable which is white in the middle and has green leaves on the outside. You usually cook a cauliflower but some people like to eat it raw.

cello

A cello is a musical instrument which looks like a big violin. To play a cello you sit down with it between your knees.

a
b
c
d
e
f
g
h
i
j
k
l
m
n
o
p
q
r
s
t
u
v
w
x
y
z

a
b
c
d
e
f
g
h
i
j
k
l
m
n
o
p
q
r
s
t
u
v
w
x
y
z

centipede

A centipede is an insect with lots of legs. It is the same size as a small worm.

chain

A chain is made of metal rings joined together.

Stephen tied his bicycle to the fence with a chain so that no one could steal it.

cheer

To cheer is to shout out loud when you are happy.

We all went to the football match to cheer our team. We wanted them to win.

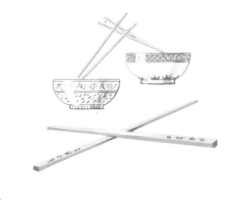

chopsticks

Chopsticks are thin wooden sticks you can use to eat with instead of a knife and fork. The Chinese and Japanese eat with chopsticks.

church

A church is a building where you go to pray and sing hymns. Most towns and villages have a church.

circle

A circle is a round shape. Wheels are always circles and so are rings which you wear on your fingers.

city

A city is a very big town. Lots of people live and work in a city and the streets are full of cars.

London is the biggest city in England.

clarinet

A clarinet is a musical instrument. You blow into it to make it play a tune.

claw

A claw is the sharp nail on the foot of a bird or animal.

An eagle uses its sharp claws to catch mice.

cliff

A cliff is a very steep hill. You often see cliffs at the seaside.

a
b
c
d
e
f
g
h
i
j
k
l
m
n
o
p
q
r
s
t
u
v
w
x
y
z

cloak

A cloak is like a coat but it does not have any sleeves.

The witch wore her cloak when she went riding on her broomstick.

clock

A clock is a machine which tells us what the time is.

Clocks have two hands and a face with numbers on it to show the hours and minutes. Clocks can be very large like Big Ben and they can also be very small.

cloud

A cloud is something you see in the sky. Clouds are made of hundreds of tiny drops of water.

There were a lot of clouds in the sky and it looked as though it was going to rain.

clown

A clown is a person you see at the circus. He does funny tricks to make people laugh.

The clown painted his face different colours and put on a false nose to make him look funny.

coat

A coat is something you wear on top of your other clothes. A coat covers your arms as well as your body.

Tom put on his coat when he went into the garden because it was cold outside.

coconut

A coconut is a very large nut. It has a thick brown shell on the outside and you can eat the white inside. Coconuts grow on palm trees.

coffee

Coffee is a hot drink. It is made from coffee beans which have been roasted and ground up.

Coffee is very dark brown and some people put milk and sugar in it.

coin

A coin is a piece of money which is made from metal. A coin has pictures on it.

He put a coin into the machine to get some chocolate.

collar

A collar is the part of your clothes which goes round your neck.

A collar can also be a strap which goes round a dog's neck. You use this to fasten the dog's lead.

comb

A comb is used to keep your hair tidy. It is made from plastic and has lots of teeth. In the old days a comb would have been made from bone.

a
b
c
d
e
f
g
h
i
j
k
l
m
n
o
p
q
r
s
t
u
v
w
x
y
z

comic

A comic is something you read. It is made from sheets of paper and has lots of pictures.

The newspaper boy brings my comic every Wednesday. I read it at once because I like it.

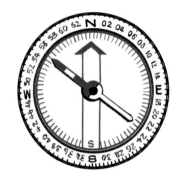

compass

A compass is an instrument which shows directions and helps you to find out where you are. A compass has a needle which can move and always points to the north. Ships have a compass to tell the captain which way he should be going.

computer

A computer is a machine which can solve problems for you.

It can store lots of information.

cork

A cork is a stopper for a bottle. You put it in the opening at the top to stop the liquid inside spilling out.

corkscrew

A corkscrew is a tool you use to get a cork out of a bottle.

corn

Corn is a plant which farmers grow in fields. The seeds of corn are ground up to make flour.

cot

A cot is a bed for a baby.

My baby sister sleeps in a cot. She is not big enough to have a bed; she would fall out of it.

cottage

A cottage is a small house in the country.

country

The country is the fields and woods which are outside towns.

A country is also all the land of one nation. England is a country.

cow

A cow is an animal which gives us milk.

Cow is also the name given to female elephants and whales.

a
b
c
d
e
f
g
h
i
j
k
l
m
n
o
p
q
r
s
t
u
v
w
x
y
z

cowboy

A cowboy is a person who rides around on a horse looking after cattle.

You often see cowboys in films on television.

crab

A crab is an animal which lives in the sea. A crab has a hard shell, four pairs of legs and one pair of claws. Some people like to cook and eat crab.

cracker

A cracker is a tube made of coloured paper. When you pull the two ends the cracker goes bang and comes apart. You find a toy or paper hat inside a cracker.

We like to have crackers at Christmas.

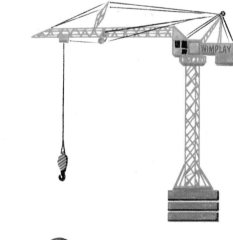

crane

A crane is a large machine which lifts heavy things. It has a long arm with a very strong chain on the end. This arm can move up and down as well as round.

A crane is also a bird with long, thin legs and a long, thin neck.

crayons

Crayons are coloured pencils or coloured sticks of wax. When you want to draw a picture you use crayons.

cricket

Cricket is a game which you play with a bat and ball and two teams of eleven people.

Cricket is also the name for an insect which is like a grasshopper.

crisps

Crisps are very thin slices of potato which have been fried. You usually buy crisps in a small bag.

crocodile

A crocodile is a long animal with short legs and a very strong tail. A crocodile has lots of sharp teeth. Crocodiles live near rivers in hot countries.

croquet

Croquet is a game played with long wooden hammers. You use these to hit wooden balls through hoops fixed in the grass.

crown

A crown is worn by a king or queen. It goes on the head and is made of gold or silver and precious jewels.

At her coronation the Queen had a crown put on her head.

a b c d e f g h i j k l m n o p q r s t u v w x y z

cucumber

A cucumber is a long vegetable which is green outside and white inside. You eat cucumber raw in a salad.

cup

A cup is a small bowl with a handle. You drink from a cup.

The cup was full of coffee.

cut

To cut means to open or divide something with a knife or scissors.

The knife was very sharp so it was easy to cut the apple in half.

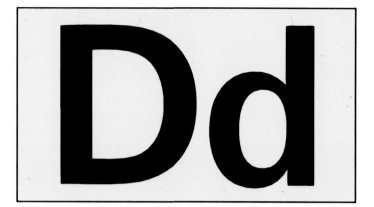

Dd

dagger

A dagger is a sharp knife like a small sword.

He stabbed the snake with a dagger and killed it.

daisy

A daisy is a small white flower which is yellow in the middle.

There were lots of daisies growing in the grass so we picked them and made a daisy chain.

dance

To dance is to move about in time to music.

Alice likes to dance and she wants to be a ballet dancer when she is older.

dark

Dark means without light.

There are no street lamps where we live so it is very dark at night. It is difficult to see where you are going.

a
b
c
d
e
f
g
h
i
j
k
l
m
n
o
p
q
r
s
t
u
v
w
x
y
z

a b c d e f g h i j k l m n o p q r s t u v w x y z

dart

A dart is a thin piece of metal with feathers at one end and a sharp point at the other. When you play darts you throw the dart into a dart board and score.

To dart means to move suddenly.

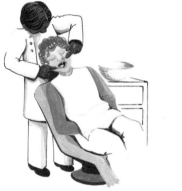

deer

A deer is a wild animal which can run very fast. Male deer have horns called antlers.

The deer was frightened when it saw the people in the woods. It ran away.

dentist

A dentist is a person who takes care of your teeth. When you have toothache you go to the dentist.

desk

A desk is a table with drawers.

The lady in the office sat at a desk to do her typing.

detective

A detective is a policeman or other person who tries to find out who the person is who has done something against the law.

The detective asked a lot of questions and soon found out who had stolen the money.

diamond

A diamond is a precious jewel that sparkles. It does not have any colour.

The Queen wears a crown which has lots of diamonds in it.

diary

A diary is a little book with all the dates of the year in it.

When Mary went on holiday she wrote down what she did each day in her diary.

dice

A dice is a cube. It has six sides with numbers one to six in dots on them.

You often use a dice when you play a game like Snakes and Ladders.

dig

To dig is to turn over the earth with a spade. You have to dig the garden to get out all the weeds.

dinosaur

A dinosaur is a very big animal which lived thousands of years ago.

You can see the skeleton of a dinosaur in a museum but you will never see a real one.

a b c d e f g h i j k l m n o p q r s t u v w x y z

a
b
c
d
e
f
g
h
i
j
k
l
m
n
o
p
q
r
s
t
u
v
w
x
y
z

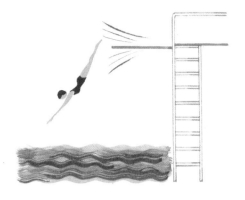

dive

To dive is to go head first into water.

Harry can dive off the highest diving-board at the swimming pool.

diver

A diver is a person who dives and works under water.

A diver wears a special suit and helmet to help him breathe when he is under water.

doctor

A doctor is someone who helps you to get better when you are ill.

The doctor came to my house when I was ill and gave me some medicine.

dog

A dog is an animal with four legs. It is often kept as a pet.

My dog barks when the postman comes to the door.

doll

A doll is a toy which looks like a small person.

dolphin

A dolphin is an animal that lives in the sea.

The dolphins in the safari park like to play with a ball in the pool.

dominoes

Dominoes is a game played between two people. It has twenty-eight little flat black bricks with white spots on. You have to match the spots.

donkey

A donkey is an animal that looks like a small horse. It has long ears and is usually grey or brown.

a
b
c
d
e
f
g
h
i
j
k
l
m
n
o
p
q
r
s
t
u
v
w
x
y
z

door

A door lets you go in and out of something.

Doors are usually made of wood but some are made of metal or glass.

dragon

A dragon is not a real animal but one you find only in story books.

The dragon in John's picture book looked very fierce.

dragonfly

A dragonfly is a large insect. It has two pairs of wings and likes to eat mosquitos.

It is very easy to see a dragonfly by the river because of its lovely colour.

drain

A drain is an opening in the ground covered with a metal grill.

When it was raining hard all the water went down the drain in the road.

To drain is to empty water from something.

We have to drain the swimming pool when it is winter.

draw

To draw is to make a picture with a pencil, crayon or pen.

drawbridge

A drawbridge is a bridge which can be moved up and down.

The soldiers went across the drawbridge into the castle. Then they raised the drawbridge so that the enemy soldiers could not follow them.

drawer

A drawer is like a box without a top. It fits into a piece of furniture and slides in and out.

Susan has lots of drawers in her bedroom and she keeps her clothes in them.

dress

A dress is a piece of clothing for women or girls. A dress can be short or long.

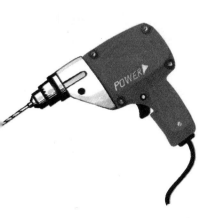

drill

A drill is a tool for making holes. It has a long pointed end which turns round and round.

Dad used his electric drill when he put up some shelves in the kitchen. He had to make holes in the wall to put in the screws.

drum

A drum is a musical instrument. It is a round hollow box with skin stretched tightly over the top and bottom. You beat a drum with two sticks and it makes a loud sound.

a b c d e f g h i j k l m n o p q r s t u v w x y z

duck

A duck is a bird which can swim. It has short legs and special feet called webbed feet.

dwarf

A dwarf is a very small person.

The dwarf could not post the letter because he could not reach the hole in the letterbox.

Ee

ear

An ear is part of your head. We all have two ears, one on each side of our head. They help us to hear all the sounds around us. If you cover up your ears with your hands you cannot hear anything.

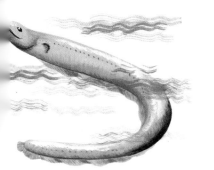

eat

To eat is to bite and swallow food.

I eat when I am hungry.

eel

An eel is a long thin fish which looks like a snake. Some people like to catch eels and eat them.

egg

An egg is something made by mother birds, fish, insects and snakes. The babies of these animals start to grow inside the eggs and then break out of them.

An egg is also a kind of food.

My hen lays an egg every day and I eat it for breakfast.

a
b
c
d
e
f
g
h
i
j
k
l
m
n
o
p
q
r
s
t
u
v
w
x
y
z

8

eight

Eight is the number which comes before nine and after seven.

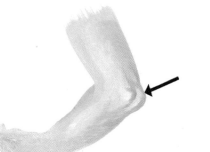

elbow

Your elbow is where your arm bends.

Your arm bends at your elbow.

elephant

An elephant is a large animal with a long nose called a trunk. An elephant has big floppy ears. If you want to ride on an elephant you have to climb up a ladder to get on.

emu

An emu is a large bird like an ostrich. An emu cannot fly but it can run very fast.

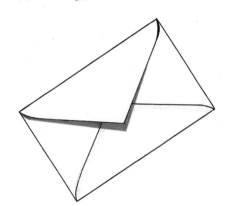

envelope

An envelope is a paper cover for a letter. When you want to send a letter to a friend you have to put a stamp on the envelope.

escalator

An escalator is a moving staircase. It is fun to go on the escalator in a big shop. It is easier than walking up lots of stairs.

eskimo

An eskimo is a person who lives in Alaska and other Arctic lands.

An eskimo wears very warm clothes nearly all the time because it is so cold.

explode

To explode is to blow up with a loud bang.

When fireworks go up into the sky they explode.

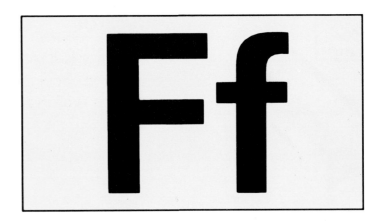

Ff

fair

A fair is lots of outdoor amusements like helter-skelters, merry-go-rounds and swings.

It is great fun to go to a fair; there is so much to do and see.

Fair is also a colour of hair. If your hair is very light and not dark it is called fair.

fairy

A fairy is a person with wings who can work magic.

Fairies are not real; you only read about them in books.

family

A father, mother and their children are called a family.

There are five people in my family: Mum, Dad, Tom, Jim and me.

fan

A fan is a machine which makes the air hot or cold.

We had to switch on the electric fan because we were so hot.

farm

A farm is a piece of land which is used for growing food or keeping animals.

If you have a holiday on a farm you can perhaps watch the farmer milking his cows.

feather

A feather is one of the soft things which grow on and cover a bird. Feathers are very light and they help to keep a bird warm. The feathers on a parrot are brightly coloured.

feet

You have two feet on the end of your legs. Each of them is called a foot.

You walk and stand up on your feet.

fight

A fight is a struggle or a battle.

The policeman had a fight with the thief. The thief did not want to get caught.

finger

Your finger is one of the five parts at the end of your hand. We use our fingers to pick up things, to write and draw and to do many other things. Some people wear rings on their fingers.

43

a
b
c
d
e
f
g
h
i
j
k
l
m
n
o
p
q
r
s
t
u
v
w
x
y
z

a
b
c
d
e
f
g
h
i
j
k
l
m
n
o
p
q
r
s
t
u
v
w
x
y
z

fire

A fire is the flames and heat made by something burning.

We made a fire near our camp so that we could cook some food and keep warm.

fire engine

A fire engine is a big motor car which takes firemen to a fire and carries all kinds of things to help put out a fire. Fire engines travel very fast.

fireman

A fireman is a person who puts fires out. Firemen wear helmets and special clothes to protect them from flames and smoke.

fireworks

Fireworks make pretty lights or a big bang when you light them with a match.

We usually have fireworks on November 5th.

My Dad would not let me light the fireworks. He said it was too dangerous.

fish

A fish is an animal which can live only in water. Fish have backbones and scales all over their bodies. They breathe through gills.

Fishermen catch fish in the sea and we cook them and eat them.

44

5

five

Five is the number before six and after four. You have five fingers on each hand.

flag

A flag is a piece of coloured material fixed to the end of a stick. Every country has a flag with a different pattern.

The children waved flags when the Queen went by.

flamingo

A flamingo is a pink or bright red bird with long legs and a long thin neck.

flute

A flute is a long thin musical instrument. When you play a flute you hold it to one side, not straight in front of you. You make sounds by covering the holes with your fingers and blowing.

fly

A fly is a small insect with wings.

To fly is to move through the air.

Aeroplanes fly, and so do birds.

a b c d e f g h i j k l m n o p q r s t u v w x y z

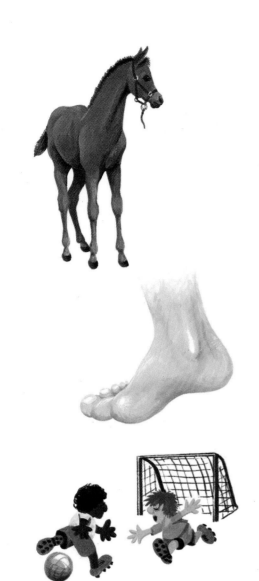

foal

A foal is a baby horse.

The baby foal looked so small when it stood by its mother.

foot

You have one foot on the end of each leg. Two of these are called feet.

football

Football is a game you play. You kick a ball into a goal.

You need twenty-two players for a real game of football.

fork

A fork is a tool used for eating. It has a handle at one end and usually four points at the other.

You can also get a very big fork and this is used to dig the garden.

fountain

A fountain is water which is made to shoot up in the air.

There is a fountain in the park. If you get too near it the water splashes over you.

4

four

Four is the number which comes before five and after three. Cows have four legs.

fox

A fox is a wild animal red-brown in colour. It looks like a dog but it has a bushy tail.

frog

A frog is a small green or brown animal which can jump a long way. Frogs can live in and out of the water.

Tim caught some tadpoles and in a few days they turned into frogs.

a
b
c
d
e
f
g
h
i
j
k
l
m
n
o
p
q
r
s
t
u
v
w
x
y
z

Gg

gate

A gate is like a door and is made of wood or metal. A gate closes an opening in a fence, wall or hedge.

If you don't shut the gate when you walk through the farmer's field, the cows will get out and the farmer will be cross.

ghost

Some people think they see dead people who have come back to earth. What they think they see is called a ghost. There are lots of stories about ghosts, but you don't have to believe them.

giant

A giant is a very very large person. You read about giants in fairy stories; they are not real people.

giraffe

A giraffe is an animal which lives in Africa. It has a long neck and long legs.

glasses

Glasses help you to see better if your eyes are weak.

gloves

Gloves are used to cover your hands and fingers when they are cold.

Elizabeth put on her gloves before she went into the garden to make a snowman.

goat

A goat is a small animal with horns. Mother goats give milk.

goose

A goose is a bird like a duck but it is bigger and has a longer neck.

The goose made a very loud noise when Jo walked into the farmyard.

grapes

Grapes are small round juicy fruits. They are black or green in colour, and grow in bunches. Grapes are used to make wine.

a
b
c
d
e
f
g
h
i
j
k
l
m
n
o
p
q
r
s
t
u
v
w
x
y
z

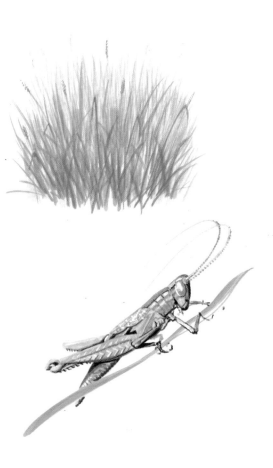

grass

Grass is the green plant which covers fields or lawns.

The grass had grown very long so my Dad cut it short with the mower.

grasshopper

A grasshopper is an insect which jumps. Grasshoppers make a chirping noise.

You could hear the grasshopper in the long grass but you could not see him.

green

Green is the colour of grass.

The grasshopper was green, so you could not see him in the grass.

greenhouse

A greenhouse is a glass house used for growing plants in. When the sun shines through the glass it is very warm inside.

guinea pig

A guinea pig is a small animal with short ears, short legs and no tail.

There was a guinea pig in the pet corner at school. He liked being stroked.

guitar

A guitar is a musical instrument with six strings. You play it by plucking the strings.

gun

A gun is a machine which shoots bullets.

The soldier had a gun in his hand.

a
b
c
d
e
f
g
h
i
j
k
l
m
n
o
p
q
r
s
t
u
v
w
x
y
z

Hh

hair

Hair is the thin threads which grow on your head. Hair grows all over the body on many animals. Hair can be lots of colours.

hammer

A hammer is a tool used for putting nails into wood and walls. A hammer has a handle with a metal head.

When Dad uses his hammer he often hits his finger and not the nail.

hamster

A hamster is a little furry animal. It can keep food in a pouch at the side of its mouth.

Our hamster likes to come out of his cage sometimes and run about the room. He is a lovely pet.

hare

A hare is an animal like a rabbit, only bigger. Hares have longer ears too.

a
b
c
d
e
f
g
h
i
j
k
l
m
n
o
p
q
r
s
t
u
v
w
x
y
z

heart

Your heart is an important part of your body. It pumps blood all round your body.

hedge

A hedge is a row of bushes planted close together. Some people have a hedge round their garden.

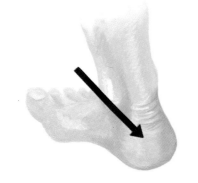

hedgehog

A hedgehog is a small animal with sharp points called prickles all over its back. It eats insects.

When the hedgehog heard me he was frightened and rolled himself up into a ball.

heel

Your heel is the back part of your foot.

helicopter

A helicopter is a kind of aeroplane with metal blades to make it fly.

We watched the helicopter fly straight up into the air. It did not need a runway.

a
b
c
d
e
f
g
h
i
j
k
l
m
n
o
p
q
r
s
t
u
v
w
x
y
z

a b c d e f g h i j k l m n o p q r s t u v w x y z

hippopotamus

A hippopotamus is a very large grey-coloured animal. It lives in or near rivers and lakes in hot countries.

A hippopotamus is very heavy.

hive

A hive is a small house which bees live in. Bees make honey in their hive.

hook

A hook is a piece of metal or plastic which is curved at one end.

John hangs his coat on a hook because his Mum does not like him to leave it lying on the floor.

hoop

A hoop is a very large ring made of wood or plastic.

The hoop went rolling very fast down the hill and no one could catch it.

hop

To hop is to jump on one leg or to make little jumps.

It makes my leg tired when I hop down the road.

horse

A horse is a large animal. You can ride on some horses or use them to pull heavy things.

house

A house is a building which people live in.

hovercraft

A hovercraft is a machine which moves across the top of water. Air is pumped out of the bottom so that the hovercraft floats just above the water.

a
b
c
d
e
f
g
h
i
j
k
l
m
n
o
p
q
r
s
t
u
v
w
x
y
z

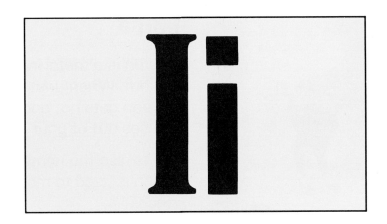

iceberg

An iceberg is a very large piece of ice which floats on water. An iceberg looks like a white mountain in the sea.

ice cream

Ice cream is a very cold frozen food. It is made from cream and sugar. Ice creams have to be kept in a freezer or else they melt.

igloo

An igloo is a house made from blocks of snow. Eskimos used to live in igloos.

When it snowed, the children made an igloo in the garden. They crawled into it and it was quite warm inside.

iron

An iron is a metal instrument with a flat bottom. When you plug it into electricity, the iron gets hot and you can use it to get creases out of your clothes.

Iron is also the name of a very strong metal which is used to make all kinds of machines.

island

An island is a piece of land with water all round it.

We had to row a boat across the water to get to the island. You could not get there by car.

a
b
c
d
e
f
g
h
i
j
k
l
m
n
o
p
q
r
s
t
u
v
w
x
y
z

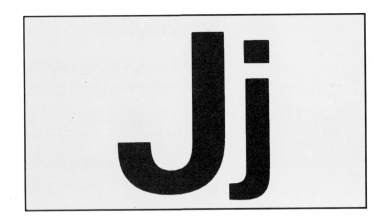

jam

Jam is a sweet food. You make it by boiling sugar and fruit together until it becomes thick.

Some people like to eat jam on bread and butter.

jar

A jar is a kind of bottle which has a wide opening at the top.

You put jam in a jar.

jeans

Jeans are blue cotton trousers. Lots of boys and girls and men and women wear jeans because they are comfortable.

jelly

Jelly is a sweet food which wobbles about. It is made from sugar and fruit juice.

There was red jelly and ice cream to eat at the birthday party.

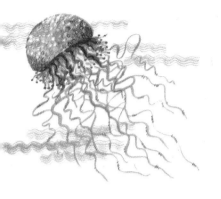

jellyfish

A jellyfish is a sea animal. Its body is soft like jelly.

jigsaw

A jigsaw is a puzzle made of lots of small pieces of cardboard or wood of all different shapes. When you put them together they make a picture.

jockey

A jockey is a person who rides a racehorse.

A jockey is a small man who is not too heavy. This means the horse can go faster.

jog

To jog is to run slowly.

Some people like to jog round the park. They think it keeps them fit.

jug

A jug is a container for liquids. It has a handle. You pour milk into a jug.

a b c d e f g h i j k l m n o p q r s t u v w x y z

a b c d e f g h i j k l m n o p q r s t u v w x y z

juggle

To juggle is to keep throwing lots of balls in the air and catching them again. A person who can juggle is called a juggler.

juice

Juice is the liquid from fruit, vegetables or meat.

It is good for you to drink real orange juice everyday.

jump

To jump is to leap into the air.

Humpty Dumpty did not jump off the wall; he fell.

junk

Junk is rubbish and all the things you throw away.

A junk is a Chinese sailing boat.

Kk

kangaroo

A kangaroo is a wild animal which lives in Australia. It has a long tail and very strong back legs. Kangaroos can hop very quickly. Mother kangaroos carry their babies in a pouch in front of them.

kennel

A kennel is a small house for a dog.

The dog's kennel is in the garden and he sleeps in it at night.

kettle

A kettle is a metal container which you use to boil water.

When Mum makes a cup of tea she boils the water in a kettle.

key

A key is a piece of metal which is cut into a special shape.

You use a key to lock and unlock doors.

a
b
c
d
e
f
g
h
i
j
k
l
m
n
o
p
q
r
s
t
u
v
w
x
y
z

kick

To kick is to hit with your foot.

Tom wears football boots when he plays football so that he can kick the ball a long way.

king

A king is a man who rules a country.

Do you know the names of any kings?

kiss

To kiss is to touch someone's face or hands with your lips.

John gave his mother a kiss because he loved her very much.

kite

A kite is a toy which is made from thin, light strips of wood and covered with paper, plastic or material. You fly a kite in the air on a very long piece of string.

kitten

A kitten is a baby cat.

Kittens like playing with a ball of wool.

a
b
c
d
e
f
g
h
i
j
k
l
m
n
o
p
q
r
s
t
u
v
w
x
y
z

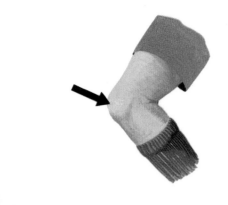

knee

Your knee is the part of your leg which bends.

kneel

To kneel is to go down on your knees.

knife

A knife is a metal tool which is used for cutting. It has a handle and is sharp on one side.

knight

A long time ago soldiers who rode horses were called knights.

a
b
c
d
e
f
g
h
i
j
k
l
m
n
o
p
q
r
s
t
u
v
w
x
y
z

knit

To knit is to make clothes from wool using long needles.

It took Sarah a long time to knit a jumper.

koala

A koala is an animal like a small bear which lives in Australia. A koala has a black nose and no tail.

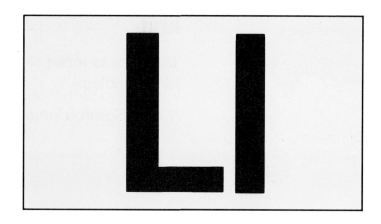

Ll

ladder

A ladder is made of pieces of wood or metal fixed between two long poles to make steps to stand on.

The window cleaner uses a ladder to climb up to the bedroom windows.

ladybird

A ladybird is a kind of small round beetle which is usually red with black spots.

You often see ladybirds on the leaves of plants.

laugh

To laugh means to make a sound to show that you are happy.

The monkeys at the zoo made me laugh. They were doing funny tricks all the time.

leaf

A leaf is the flat green part of a tree or plant.

a
b
c
d
e
f
g
h
i
j
k
l
m
n
o
p
q
r
s
t
u
v
w
x
y
z

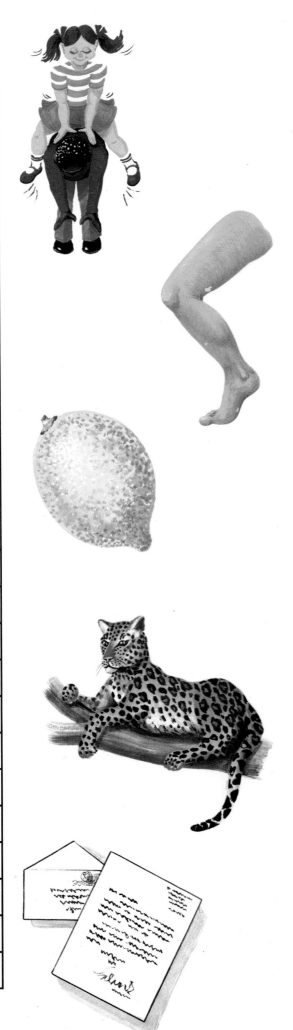

leap

To leap is to jump.

When you play leap frog you jump over another person who is bending down.

leg

Your legs are the part of your body you use to stand and walk on. You have two legs.

lemon

A lemon is a sour yellow fruit. Lemons grow in hot countries on small trees.

leopard

A leopard is a wild animal like a large cat. It has yellow fur with black spots and lives in Africa.

letter

A letter is a piece of paper with writing on it which you send by post in an envelope to someone.

Words are made with letters.

66

lettuce

A lettuce is a plant with large, green leaves. You eat lettuce in a salad.

lick

To lick is to touch with your tongue.

Alison licks the lollipop.

lifeboat

A lifeboat is a special kind of boat which is used to help other boats which are in trouble at sea.

The lifeboat went out to sea quickly because a boat was sinking. It saved the lives of all the crew.

lighthouse

A lighthouse is a tall building near, or in, the sea. It has a bright light at the top which flashes on and off to warn ships of dangerous rocks in the sea.

lightning

Lightning is a flash of light in the sky. You usually see lightning in a thunderstorm.

Helen heard the thunder and saw the lightning and she knew it would soon pour with rain.

a b c d e f g h i j k l m n o p q r s t u v w x y z

67

a
b
c
d
e
f
g
h
i
j
k
l
m
n
o
p
q
r
s
t
u
v
w
x
y
z

lion

A lion is a wild animal like a large cat which lives mainly in Africa.

lizard

A lizard is a little animal with a long tail and short legs.

You can sometimes see lizards on the sand dunes near the sea.

log

A log is a thick piece of wood from a tree.

We made a lovely fire with logs we had found in the wood.

lollipop

A lollipop is a sweet or an ice cream on the end of a stick.

lorry

A lorry is a large vehicle which is used to carry heavy things.

When we were driving on the motorway a lorry passed us. It was carrying a big load of fruit.

luggage

Luggage is all the suitcases and bags you take with you when you go on holiday.

When we put all the luggage into the car there was no room for us.

a
b
c
d
e
f
g
h
i
j
k
l
m
n
o
p
q
r
s
t
u
v
w
x
y
z

a
b
c
d
e
f
g
h
i
j
k
l
m
n
o
p
q
r
s
t
u
v
w
x
y
z

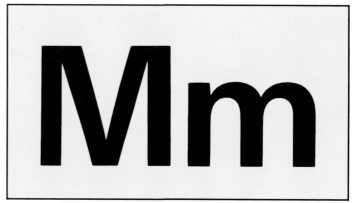

Mm

magnet

A magnet is a special piece of metal which can pull other metals towards it.

When all the pins fell on the carpet, Jane used a magnet to pick them up.

magnifying glass

A magnifying glass is a special glass which makes things look bigger than they really are.

The insect was so tiny that Alice had to look at it through her magnifying glass to see it clearly.

march

To march is to walk in step with other people.

The soldiers marched up the street.

March is also the third month of the year.

marmalade

Marmalade is a sweet food like jam. It is made from oranges, lemons or grapefruit.

We have marmalade on our toast at breakfast time.

medal

A medal is a piece of metal like a big coin. You are sometimes given a medal if you do something very brave.

The fireman was given a medal because he rescued a baby from a big fire.

microscope

A microscope is an instrument which helps us to see very small things because it makes them look bigger.

midnight

Midnight is twelve o'clock at night.

Tom would love to stay up until midnight but his Dad says it is too late.

mirror

A mirror is a flat shiny piece of glass. You can see yourself in a mirror.

mittens

Mittens are gloves without fingers.

My baby sister wears mittens because they are easier to put on than gloves.

a
b
c
d
e
f
g
h
i
j
k
l
m
n
o
p
q
r
s
t
u
v
w
x
y
z

a
b
c
d
e
f
g
h
i
j
k
l
m
n
o
p
q
r
s
t
u
v
w
x
y
z

mole

A mole is a little animal that lives under the ground. It uses its long front claws to dig tunnels.

monkey

A monkey is a small animal with a long tail and very long arms and legs. Monkeys are clever animals.

mosquito

A mosquito is a small flying insect which can bite or sting you. Some mosquitos carry germs and can make you ill.

mouse

A mouse is a small furry animal with a long tail. A mouse can live outside or in a house.

My cat caught a mouse and ate it.

mug

A mug is a big cup.

Jennifer has her coffee in a mug because she likes a lot of it.

mushroom

A mushroom is a little plant which looks like a white umbrella. You can eat some mushrooms but some of the ones you see growing in woods and fields are poisonous and will make you ill.

a
b
c
d
e
f
g
h
i
j
k
l
m
n
o
p
q
r
s
t
u
v
w
x
y
z

a
b
c
d
e
f
g
h
i
j
k
l
m
n
o
p
q
r
s
t
u
v
w
x
y
z

Nn

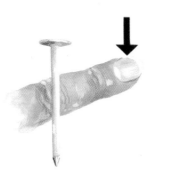

nail

A nail is a thin piece of metal with a sharp point at one end and a flat top at the other.

A nail is also the hard part at the end of your fingers and toes.

nest

A nest is a home which is built by a bird. It is made from grass, twigs, leaves and other things.

There is a nest in the hedge with five eggs in it. We are looking at it carefully but not touching it.

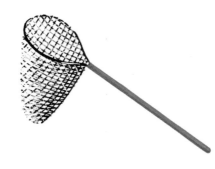

net

A net is made from pieces of string which have been knotted together.

Peter uses a net to catch fish.

newspaper

A newspaper is sheets of thin paper with printing and pictures on them. A newspaper tells you news or what has happened in the world.

Pam buys a newspaper every morning.

newt

A newt is a small animal which lives in or near water. It looks a bit like a lizard.

9

nine

Nine is the number which comes before ten and after eight.

noon

Noon is twelve o'clock in the daytime. It is the middle of the day.

At noon the sun is high in the sky and it is the hottest time of the day.

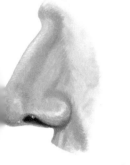

nose

You breathe through your nose and smell with it. Your nose is part of your face.

nurse

A nurse is a person who looks after sick people.

When Simon went to hospital to have his tonsils out, the nurses were very kind to him.

a
b
c
d
e
f
g
h
i
j
k
l
m
n
o
p
q
r
s
t
u
v
w
x
y
z

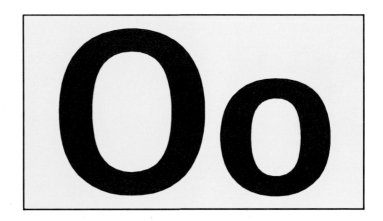

a
b
c
d
e
f
g
h
i
j
k
l
m
n
o
p
q
r
s
t
u
v
w
x
y
z

Oo

oboe

An oboe is a long, thin musical instrument. You play it by putting one end in your mouth and blowing.

octopus

An octopus is an animal which lives in the sea. It has a soft body and eight arms called tentacles. An octopus moves along the bottom of the sea.

one

One is the first number. It comes before two.

onion

An onion is a vegetable which has a brown skin and is white inside. It has a very strong taste and smell.

orange

An orange is a sweet fruit. It has a thick skin which you peel off before you eat the soft juicy part inside.

Orange is also a colour.

ostrich

An ostrich is a very large bird which lives in Africa. Although it is a bird it cannot fly, but it can run very fast.

otter

An otter is a small brown animal which lives in and near rivers.

owl

An owl is a bird with big eyes. It sleeps in the daytime and hunts for food at night. Owls like to eat mice, frogs and insects.

a b c d e f g h i j k l m n o p q r s t u v w x y z

a
b
c
d
e
f
g
h
i
j
k
l
m
n
o
p
q
r
s
t
u
v
w
x
y
z

Pp

paddle

A paddle is a long, thin piece of wood with a flat, wide end. You use a paddle to make a boat move in the water.

To paddle is to walk in water without shoes.

pancake

A pancake is a flat, thin cake. You cook it in hot fat in a frying pan.

panda

A panda is a large black and white animal like a bear which lives in China.

Everyone enjoyed watching the panda eat bamboo shoots at the zoo.

panther

A panther is a black leopard.

parachute

A parachute is a large piece of cloth with strings which looks like an umbrella. When you jump from an aeroplane in the sky you use a parachute. You are tied to it with ropes and it helps you to come down slowly to the ground.

parcel

A parcel is anything wrapped up in paper.

The postman brought some parcels on my birthday.

park

A park is a special place you go to play in. Parks have grass, flowers and trees and sometimes swings.

parrot

A parrot is a bird with brightly coloured feathers. You can teach parrots to talk, so some people keep them as pets.

a
b
c
d
e
f
g
h
i
j
k
l
m
n
o
p
q
r
s
t
u
v
w
x
y
z

a
b
c
d
e
f
g
h
i
j
k
l
m
n
o
p
q
r
s
t
u
v
w
x
y
z

patchwork

Patchwork is lots of small pieces of material sewn together.

There was a pretty patchwork cover in the baby's cot.

path

A path is a place for walking. Cars must not go on to the path; they must keep to the road.

peach

A peach is a sweet fruit with an orange-pink skin. The skin of a peach feels like velvet when you touch it.

peacock

A peacock is a large bird with a beautiful blue and green tail.

pear

A pear is a sweet green or yellow juicy fruit which grows on a tree.

peas

Peas are soft, small green seeds which grow in a pod. You can cook the seeds or eat them raw.

pebbles

Pebbles are small round stones.

Walking on the pebbles at the seaside made my bare feet sore.

peel

Peel is the skin of fruit or vegetables.

To peel is to take this skin off.

Most people do not like to eat the peel of a banana so they peel it off.

peg

A peg is a piece of wood or plastic which fixes clothes on a washing line.

pelican

A pelican is a big bird with a large bill and webbed feet. It has a large pouch under its bill which is used to carry fish.

a b c d e f g h i j k l m n o p q r s t u v w x y z

pen

A pen is a tool used for writing in ink.

A pen is also a small space with a fence all round used for keeping pigs or sheep in.

penguin

A penguin is a big black and white sea bird which lives near the South Pole. Penguins cannot fly but they can swim.

penknife

A penknife is a small knife. The blades can be folded so that you can carry the knife in your pocket safely.

photograph

A photograph is a picture made by a camera.

piano

A piano is a large musical instrument. When you press down on the keys of a piano, they move little hammers at the back so that they hit the metal strings. This is how a tune is made.

a
b
c
d
e
f
g
h
i
j
k
l
m
n
o
p
q
r
s
t
u
v
w
x
y
z

pie

A pie is a food. It has pastry on the outside and fruit or meat inside. You bake a pie in the oven before you eat it.

pig

A pig is a pink, farm animal with a curly tail and short legs.

pigeon

A pigeon is a grey bird with short legs. You often see pigeons in the cities as well as in the country and some people keep them in their gardens in a pigeon house.

pillow

A pillow is a bag filled with something soft like feathers. When you go to bed, you put your head on a pillow and it helps to make you comfortable.

pilot

A pilot is a person who flies an aeroplane.

The pilot let me sit at the front of the aeroplane with him.

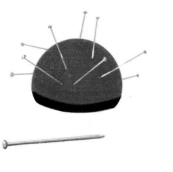

pin

A pin is a small piece of metal with a sharp point at one end.

You use a pin to hold together material or paper.

pineapple

A pineapple is a large fruit which grows in hot countries. The outside of a pineapple is very hard and prickly. The inside is yellow and juicy and lovely to eat.

pink

Pink is the colour you make when you mix red and white in your paint box.

pipe

A pipe is a tube or a long piece of metal, plastic or rubber with a hole through the middle.

Water and gas come into your home through pipes in the ground.

A pipe is also a small tube with a bowl at the end used for smoking tobacco.

pirate

A pirate is a person who attacks ships and steals things from them.

The pirates came on board the ship and stole the treasure.

plane

A plane is a tool you use to make wood smooth.

The wood was very rough with lots of splinters so my Dad used his plane to make it smooth.

plate

A plate is a flat dish. You put food on a plate.

pliers

Pliers are used for holding or bending things.

Dad keeps his pliers in his tool box.

plug

A plug is a piece of rubber or plastic which you use to fill a hole.

Ann put the plug in the bath to stop the water running out.

A plug is also a small plastic object with metal pins which you find on all electrical machines. It connects them to electricity.

plum

A plum is a purple or red juicy fruit which has a stone in the middle.

We picked lots of plums off the tree and made them into jam.

a
b
c
d
e
f
g
h
i
j
k
l
m
n
o
p
q
r
s
t
u
v
w
x
y
z

plumber

A plumber is a person who mends water pipes.

The radiator was leaking so the plumber came to mend it.

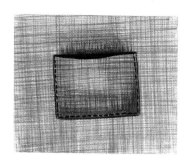

pocket

A pocket is a little bag for holding things which is sewn into trousers and other clothes.

Tom put his money into his trouser pocket.

policeman

A policeman is a person who sees that we do not do anything against the law.

The policeman stopped the driver because he was going too fast.

poncho

A poncho is a kind of clothing like a blanket with a hole in the middle of it for your head to go through.

poodle

A poodle is a kind of dog which has very short curly hair.

poppy

A poppy is a red flower. You see poppies growing wild in fields or you can grow them from seeds in your garden.

porthole

A porthole is a round window in the side of a ship.

postman

A postman is a person who delivers letters and parcels.

On my birthday the postman could not put all the cards and parcels through the letterbox so he had to ring the bell.

potato

A potato is a vegetable which grows in the ground. Chips and crisps are made from potatoes.

pour

To pour is to make liquid run out of a jug or bottle by tipping it forward.

When Helen makes a cup of tea she pours the milk into the cup first.

a
b
c
d
e
f
g
h
i
j
k
l
m
n
o
p
q
r
s
t
u
v
w
x
y
z

a b c d e f g h i j k l m n o p q r s t u v w x y z

pram

A pram is a vehicle with four wheels used to carry babies and small children.

Tom likes to push the pram when all the family go for a walk.

prince

A prince is the son of a king or queen.

princess

A princess is the daughter of a king or queen. A princess is also the wife of a prince.

Do you know the name of a princess?

propeller

A propeller is the part of an aeroplane or boat which moves air or water so that the vehicle can move forward.

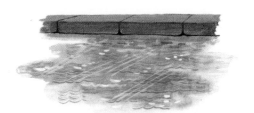

puddle

A puddle is a small pool of water.

After the thunderstorm the road was full of puddles and we had fun splashing in them.

pumpkin

A pumpkin is a large fruit. It has an orange-coloured hard skin but it is soft and juicy inside.

puppet

A puppet is a doll which can be moved either by pulling strings or by putting your hand inside, like a glove.

We all made puppets at school and acted a story with them.

pyjamas

Pyjamas are the jacket and trousers you sometimes wear in bed. Girls and boys wear pyjamas but only girls wear nightdresses.

a
b
c
d
e
f
g
h
i
j
k
l
m
n
o
p
q
r
s
t
u
v
w
x
y
z

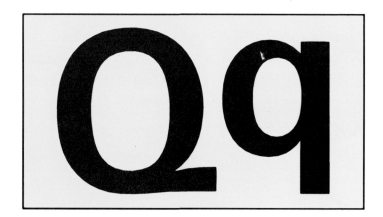

a
b
c
d
e
f
g
h
i
j
k
l
m
n
o
p
q
r
s
t
u
v
w
x
y
z

quarter

A quarter is one of four equal parts of anything. If you cut a cake into four parts all the same size, each piece is a quarter.

queen

A queen is a woman who rules a country. A queen is also the wife of a king.

question

A question is something somebody wants to know an answer to.

'What is the time?' is a question.

queue

A queue is a line of people waiting for something.

There was a queue of people by the road. They were waiting for a bus.

quill

A quill is a pen made from a feather.

Before modern pens were invented, people used to write with quills.

quoit

A quoit is a rubber or plastic ring. You throw it over a post or hook in a game.

a
b
c
d
e
f
g
h
i
j
k
l
m
n
o
p
q
r
s
t
u
v
w
x
y
z

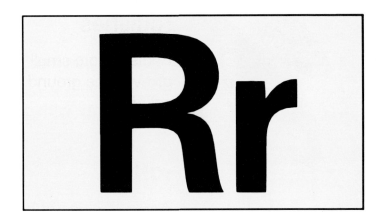

Rr

rabbit

A rabbit is a small furry animal with long ears. Most rabbits are wild but some people keep them as pets.

We watched a rabbit digging a hole in the bank. It was making a burrow to live in.

raccoon

A raccoon is a small wild animal which lives in America. It has a long, striped, bushy tail.

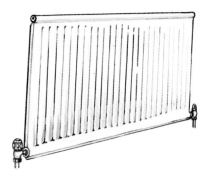

radiator

A radiator is made of metal and is used for keeping rooms warm. It is made of pipes and hot water or steam passes through these.

No one had switched the central heating on so the radiators were cold.

radio

A radio is an instrument which brings you music and voices through the air from a long way away.

If you want to, you can listen to music all day on the radio.

radishes

Radishes are small red vegetables which grow in the ground. You eat them raw in salads.

raft

A raft is a kind of boat without sides which is made of logs fixed together.

When Robin was living by a lake he made a raft so that he could sail across to the other side.

rain

Rain is the drops of water which fall from clouds.

If you go out in the rain you will get very wet.

rainbow

A rainbow is the lovely coloured arch you sometimes see in the sky when the sun is shining and it is raining at the same time.

When Mary looked up at the rainbow she counted seven different colours.

rake

A rake is a garden tool which has a long handle with plastic or metal points at the end of it.

In the Autumn, when all the leaves fall, Uncle Jim uses a rake to clear them up.

a
b
c
d
e
f
g
h
i
j
k
l
m
n
o
p
q
r
s
t
u
v
w
x
y
z

raspberry

A raspberry is a small, soft, juicy, red fruit which grows on bushes.

rat

A rat is an animal which looks like a large mouse.

Paul saw a rat in the old barn so he ran away; he did not like rats.

rattle

A rattle is a toy for a baby. It makes a noise when you shake it.

The baby played with the rattle in his pram. He liked the noise it made.

recorder

A recorder is a musical instrument which you blow into to make a sound.

record player

A record player is a machine which plays records.

Jane has a record player in her bedroom so that she can listen to music in bed.

red

Red is a colour. Lots of things you see are red: poppies, fire engines and your blood.

refrigerator

A refrigerator is a cold, metal machine like a cupboard. You keep food in it.

If you put the milk into the refrigerator it will be lovely and cold when you want to drink it.

reindeer

A reindeer is like a deer. It lives in cold countries and has large horns which are called antlers.

restaurant

A restaurant is a place you go to, to eat food which you pay for.

As a birthday treat, all my friends came to a restaurant with me for tea. My Dad paid the bill.

rhinoceros

A rhinoceros is a big wild animal with a thick skin and one or two horns on its nose. It lives in Africa or Asia.

a b c d e f g h i j k l m n o p q r s t u v w x y z

a
b
c
d
e
f
g
h
i
j
k
l
m
n
o
p
q
r
s
t
u
v
w
x
y
z

rice

Rice is the seed of a plant which grows in hot countries. Rice is very hard but when you cook it to eat it becomes soft.

rock

A rock is a very big stone.

We sat on the rocks at the seaside.

rocket

A rocket is a machine which goes into space. When a rocket is launched it goes straight up into the sky.

A rocket is also a special kind of firework which shoots up into the sky.

rocking chair

A rocking chair is a chair with curved pieces of wood under the legs to make it move backwards and forwards.

When Gran sat in her rocking chair she soon fell asleep.

roller skates

Roller skates are like shoes with little wheels on the bottom. You fit roller skates to your ordinary shoes so that you can move quickly.

96

rolling pin

A rolling pin is a long round piece of wood which is used to roll out pastry to make it flat.

roof

A roof is the top part of a building.

The cat climbed on to the roof of our house. He could not get down because it was so high.

rose

A rose is a flower which has a sweet smell. Roses can be red, pink, yellow or white. The bushes they grow on are very prickly.

rubbish

Rubbish is anything which is useless or which has been thrown away.

We burnt a lot of rubbish on the bonfire; it was lots of old newspapers.

a
b
c
d
e
f
g
h
i
j
k
l
m
n
o
p
q
r
s
t
u
v
w
x
y
z

a
b
c
d
e
f
g
h
i
j
k
l
m
n
o
p
q
r
s
t
u
v
w
x
y
z

rug

A rug is a very small carpet.

Judy has a rug by the side of her bed. It stops her feet getting cold when she gets up.

run

To run is to go very quickly. You have to run very fast if you want to win a race.

Ss

sailor

A sailor is a person who works on a ship. A sailor usually wears a uniform.

sand

Sand is what you find at the seaside or in the desert. It is little bits of rock which have broken up.

sandwich

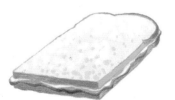

A sandwich is two pieces of bread with some food in the middle.

My favourite sandwich has peanut butter in it.

saucer

A saucer is a flat dish. You stand a cup on a saucer.

a b c d e f g h i j k l m n o p q r s t u v w x y z

sausage

A sausage is made from meat that has been chopped up and put into a tube.

We cooked some sausages on the barbeque and ate them.

saxophone

A saxophone is a musical instrument which you blow into made from shiny metal.

scales

You use scales to find out how heavy something is.

When Alec made a cake he weighed the flour on the scales.

scarecrow

A scarecrow is an object made to look like a person, and is put into a field to frighten birds away so that they will not eat seeds.

We made a scarecrow with our old clothes and gave him to the farmer.

scarf

A scarf is a piece of cloth which you wear round your neck.

Ann put on her scarf because she was cold.

school

A school is a place where children go to learn. In this country all children go to school when they are five.

scissors

Scissors are used for cutting. They have two handles and two sharp blades.

Angela wanted to make a dress so she cut out the material with sharp scissors.

screw

A screw is like a thick nail. It is made of metal. You turn it round and round with a screwdriver to make it go into a wall or a piece of wood.

scrub

To scrub is to make something clean by rubbing it hard with a brush.

The dog made dirty marks on the kitchen floor, so Mum had to scrub it.

sea

The sea is the salt water which covers part of the Earth.

Our caravan is parked near the sea.

We like to take our boat for a sail on the sea.

a b c d e f g h i j k l m n o p q r s t u v w x y z

sea horse

A sea horse is a kind of little fish. Its head looks a bit like a horse's head.

seal

A seal is an animal which usually lives in the sea. Seals can also live on land and they do this when they have young babies to look after.

seat belt

A seat belt is a strap in a car which stops you from falling out or being hurt if the car crashes. It is against the law not to wear a seat belt.

seesaw

A seesaw is a long piece of metal or wood which is put over something so that when one end goes up the other goes down.

Bill likes to go to the park with his friends to play on the seesaw.

seven

7

Seven is the number which comes before eight and after six.

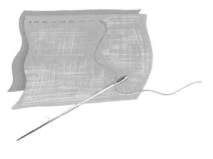

sew

To sew is to join material together with a needle and thread.

shark

A shark is a big fish that lives in the sea. A shark eats other fish and sometimes attacks people.

shed

A shed is a little wooden building.

We have a shed in our garden and we keep the garden tools and lawn-mower in it.

sheep

A sheep is a farm animal. We use the thick coat of a sheep to make wool.

sheet

A sheet is a piece of thin cloth which covers a bed.

The sheet on my bed has pretty flowers on it.

a
b
c
d
e
f
g
h
i
j
k
l
m
n
o
p
q
r
s
t
u
v
w
x
y
z

a
b
c
d
e
f
g
h
i
j
k
l
m
n
o
p
q
r
s
t
u
v
w
x
y
z

shelf

A shelf is a piece of wood fixed to the wall so that you can put things on it.

shell

A shell is something you find on the beach.

A shell is also the outside of eggs and nuts. Some animals and insects have a shell on the outside of their body. Tortoises, beetles and snails all have shells.

shield

A shield is a flat piece of metal. Many years ago soldiers used to carry shields in front of them in battles to stop arrows hitting them.

shirt

A shirt is a piece of clothing which you wear on the top part of your body. A shirt usually has a collar and sleeves.

shoes

Shoes are worn on your feet. They are made of plastic or leather.

If you don't put your shoes on, your feet will hurt when you walk on the pebbles on the beach.

shop

A shop is a place where you go to buy things.

shoulder

Your shoulder is the place where your arm joins your body.

shower

A shower is something fixed in a bathroom which sprays water down on top of you.

A shower is also just a little fall of rain.

sink

A sink is the place in your kitchen where you put dirty dishes to wash them clean.

six

Six is the number which comes before seven and after five. Six is sometimes called half a dozen.

a
b
c
d
e
f
g
h
i
j
k
l
m
n
o
p
q
r
s
t
u
v
w
x
y
z

a
b
c
d
e
f
g
h
i
j
k
l
m
n
o
p
q
r
s
t
u
v
w
x
y
z

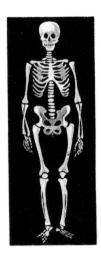

skeleton

A skeleton is the name for all the bones in your body.

skis

Skis are long, thin pieces of wood. You fix these on your boots so that you can slide over the snow.

skyscraper

A skyscraper is a very tall building.

sleigh

A sleigh is a small vehicle which has strips of metal instead of wheels.

Sleighs are built to travel over snow and ice and are pulled by horses or dogs.

slide

A slide is a big toy which is very smooth so that you can slide down it.

smoke

Smoke is what you see when something is burning.

There was a lot of smoke in the garden because Dad was having a bonfire.

snail

A snail is a small animal with a shell on its back.

Snails creep along very slowly; you often find them in the garden.

snake

A snake is a long, thin animal without legs which moves along the ground. Some snakes bite and kill people but lots of snakes are quite harmless.

snooker

Snooker is a game played on a table which is covered with green cloth. You hit coloured balls into pockets with a long stick called a cue.

snow

Snow is tiny frozen drops of water which fall in cold weather.

a
b
c
d
e
f
g
h
i
j
k
l
m
n
o
p
q
r
s
t
u
v
w
x
y
z

snowman

A snowman is something you make with snow for fun.

It is snow made into the shape of a man.

soap

Soap is used with water. You rub it on your hands or clothes to make them clean.

socks

Socks are the clothes we put on our feet before we put our shoes on.

Tom was given some new football socks for his birthday.

soldier

A soldier is a person who is in the army.

We knew the man was a soldier because he was wearing a uniform.

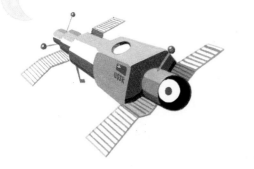

spacecraft

A spacecraft is a special kind of vehicle which can travel in outer space.

spade

A spade is a tool which is used for digging.

spaghetti

Spaghetti is a food which looks like long pieces of string. You need to cook spaghetti before you eat it.

spider

A spider is an insect with eight legs.

Spiders make webs and catch flies in them to eat.

squirrel

A squirrel is a small animal with a long bushy tail. Most squirrels are grey. They like to eat nuts.

stable

A stable is a house for horses.

In the Winter the horse sleeps in its stable because it is warmer than in the field.

a
b
c
d
e
f
g
h
i
j
k
l
m
n
o
p
q
r
s
t
u
v
w
x
y
z

stairs

Stairs are the steps inside a building which let you go from one floor to another. To get to the bedrooms in a house you often go up the stairs.

stamp

A stamp is a small piece of paper which you buy at the post office.

Before George posted the letter he stuck a stamp on it.

star

A star is a small bright light in the sky at night.

When we went for a walk in the dark we tried to count the stars, but there were too many of them.

starfish

A starfish is a fish shaped like a star.

steam roller

A steam roller is a large, heavy vehicle with a roller at the front and two big wheels at the back. A steam roller is used to help make roads.

a
b
c
d
e
f
g
h
i
j
k
l
m
n
o
p
q
r
s
t
u
v
w
x
y
z

stethoscope

A stethoscope is an instrument doctors use to listen to your heart beat.

stool

A stool is a chair without a back. Some stools have three legs.

We sit on stools in our kitchen.

strawberry

A strawberry is a sweet, red, juicy fruit. Strawberries grow on plants on the ground.

sun

The sun is the bright ball you see in the sky during the day. Without the sun, it would be cold and dark.

supermarket

A supermarket is a very big shop which sells lots of things.

a
b
c
d
e
f
g
h
i
j
k
l
m
n
o
p
q
r
s
t
u
v
w
x
y
z

surf board

A surf board is a flat piece of wood or plastic. You stand or lie on it and ride on the waves at the seaside.

swan

A swan is a large white bird with a long neck and orange beak which lives on lakes and rivers.

sweets

Sweets are made from sugar and chocolate. Eating too many sweets is bad for your teeth.

swim

To swim is to move along in the water by using your arms and legs. It is good exercise to swim in the pool every day.

switch

A switch is what you use to turn things on and off.

sword

A sword is a long, thin piece of metal with a sharp point, like a very sharp knife.

Long ago soldiers used swords in battles, but now they use guns.

a
b
c
d
e
f
g
h
i
j
k
l
m
n
o
p
q
r
s
t
u
v
w
x
y
z

a
b
c
d
e
f
g
h
i
j
k
l
m
n
o
p
q
r
s
t
u
v
w
x
y
z

Tt

table

A table is a piece of furniture. It has a flat top and four legs.

tadpole

A tadpole is a young frog. It does not have legs at first but grows them before it becomes a proper frog.

tail

A tail is the part of an animal which grows out of the back.

How many different animals with tails can you draw?

tank

A tank is a very strong vehicle which has guns on it.

A tank is also a container for liquids.

We went to the garage to put petrol in the tank of our car.

tap

A tap is a kind of handle which you turn to make water flow or to stop it.

Susan turned the tap on and washed her hands.

tape recorder

A tape recorder is a machine for playing tapes or recording music on tape.

taxi

A taxi is a car with a driver which you pay to ride in.

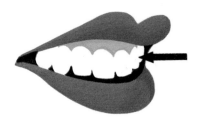

teeth

Teeth are the hard white things in your mouth. You bite with your teeth.

When my teeth ache I go to the dentist.

telephone

A telephone is an instrument which carries your voice through electric wires so that you can talk to someone a long way away.

a
b
c
d
e
f
g
h
i
j
k
l
m
n
o
p
q
r
s
t
u
v
w
x
y
z

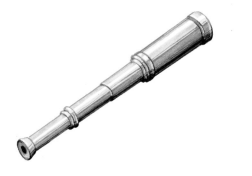

telescope

A telescope is an instrument which helps you see things which are a long way away.

Telescopes are very useful if you want to look at stars in the sky.

television

Television is an instrument which brings you pictures and sounds from a long way away.

ten

Ten is the number which comes before eleven and after nine. You have ten fingers and ten toes.

tent

A tent is a house made of material that you can fold up.

thermos

A thermos is a container which keeps liquids hot or cold.

thimble

A thimble is a small piece of metal or plastic which fits over the top of your finger. This stops the needle hurting you when you are sewing.

thistle

A thistle is a plant which has prickly leaves and purple flowers.

three

3

Three is the number which comes before four and after two.

A bicycle with three wheels is called a tricycle.

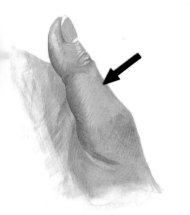

thumb

Your thumb is the shortest, thickest finger on your hand.

ticket

A ticket is a small piece of paper which you get when you pay to go somewhere.

Mike gave the bus conductor ten pence and the conductor gave him a ticket.

MIDLAND BUS COMPANY
364884
Half
Fare
10p Single
364884

tiger

A tiger is a large wild animal like a big cat, which lives in Asia.

A tiger has an orange coat with black stripes.

toast

Toast is a slice of bread which has been made brown and crunchy by heating. Many people eat toast for breakfast.

tomato

A tomato is a soft, round, red fruit. Tomatoes grow on bushes, usually in a greenhouse. You can eat tomatoes raw or cooked.

tongue

Your tongue is the pink part of your body inside your mouth which moves around. Your tongue helps you to taste your food.

toothpaste

Toothpaste is the paste which you put on to your toothbrush to clean your teeth with.

Toothpaste comes in a tube.

tortoise

A tortoise is an animal. It has four short legs and a thick shell which covers its body.

Tortoises can live in fresh water or on land.

towel

A towel is a piece of cloth which you use to dry things that are wet.

tractor

A tractor is a heavy machine with big wheels. Farmers use tractors to pull heavy loads.

train

A train is several railway coaches pulled by an engine.

tree

A tree is a tall plant with a trunk, branches and leaves.

a
b
c
d
e
f
g
h
i
j
k
l
m
n
o
p
q
r
s
t
u
v
w
x
y
z

a
b
c
d
e
f
g
h
i
j
k
l
m
n
o
p
q
r
s
t
u
v
w
x
y
z

triangle

A triangle is a shape with three sides.

tricycle

A tricycle is a bicycle with three wheels.

turkey

A turkey is a bird like a large chicken.

We sometimes eat turkey at Christmas.

turtle

A turtle is an animal which looks like a large tortoise. It can live on land and in water.

2

two

Two is the number which comes before three and after one.

typewriter

A typewriter is a machine that prints letters when you press the keys. If you want a letter to look very neat you use a typewriter.

a
b
c
d
e
f
g
h
i
j
k
l
m
n
o
p
q
r
s
t
u
v
w
x
y
z

Uu

a b c d e f g h i j k l m n o p q r s t u v w x y z

umbrella

An umbrella is something you use to stop you from getting wet in the rain.

unicorn

A unicorn is a make-believe animal which looks like a horse with a horn.

You read about unicorns in story books.

Upside down
ABC

upside down

Upside down is the wrong way up.

122

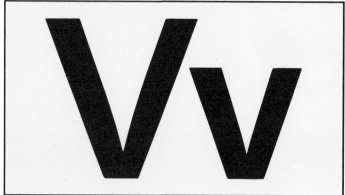

Vv

vacuum cleaner

A vacuum cleaner is a machine which runs by electricity. It sucks up dirt from carpets.

vase

A vase is a container for keeping flowers in.

Mary picked some flowers in the garden and put them in a vase full of water.

vegetables

Vegetables are plants which are grown for food.

How many vegetables can you name?

vet

A vet is a doctor who looks after animals.

When our cat had a thorn in his paw we took him to the vet.

a
b
c
d
e
f
g
h
i
j
k
l
m
n
o
p
q
r
s
t
u
v
w
x
y
z

video recorder

A video recorder is a machine which can record a programme from television and play it back later.

violin

A violin is a musical instrument. It has four strings and you hold it under your chin and play it with a bow.

volcano

A volcano is a mountain with a hole in the top of it. Sometimes flames and steam shoot out of the top. When this happens hot ashes roll down the side of the volcano.

vulture

A vulture is a large bird which eats dead animals.

Ww

waist

Your waist is the middle of your body. You put a belt round your waist.

wall

A wall is built from bricks or stones. A wall can be the side of a building or it can be a brick fence.

wallet

A wallet is a little, flat case which you use to keep money in.

walrus

A walrus is a large sea animal with two white tusks which lives in the Arctic where it is cold.

a b c d e f g h i j k l m n o p q r s t u v w x y z

wardrobe

A wardrobe is a cupboard for hanging clothes in. Most people have a wardrobe in their bedroom.

wasp

A wasp is an insect like a bee. It has black and yellow stripes.

Colin sat on a wasp by mistake and it stung him.

watch

A watch is a small clock. You wear it round your wrist or put it in your pocket. It tells you the time.

To watch is to look at carefully.

We like to watch the birds eating the nuts at the bird table.

waterfall

A waterfall is a place where water falls from a high place over rocks or cliffs.

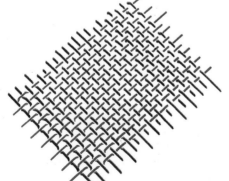

weave

To weave is to make material from cotton or wool.

wedding

A wedding is the time when two people get married.

Susan went to the church to see her sister's wedding.

weep

To weep is to cry.

Sometimes when you feel unhappy you weep.

whale

A whale is the biggest sea animal.

wheel

A wheel is like a hoop. Most vehicles cannot move without wheels. Tractors have very large wheels and model cars have very small ones.

wheelbarrow

A wheelbarrow is a little cart with one wheel and two handles.

a b c d e f g h i j k l m n o p q r s t u v w x y z

white

White is the colour of clean snow.

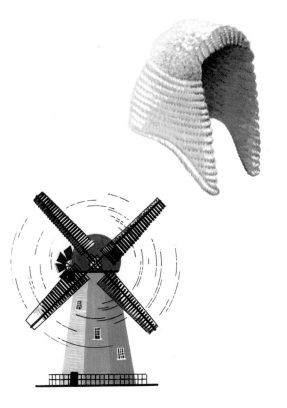

wig

A wig is a covering for your head which is made from hair.

windmill

A windmill is a building with sails on the outside which are turned round by the wind. These move a machine inside which grinds up corn into flour.

witch

A witch is a woman who has magic powers.

The fairy story I am reading is all about a witch and her magic spells.

wizard

A wizard is a man who has magic powers.

a b c d e f g h i j k l m n o p q r s t u v w x y z

wolf

A wolf is a wild animal which looks like a dog.

Which fairy story do you know that has a wolf in it?

worm

A worm is a small thin animal without legs, a bit like a tiny snake.

When you dig the garden you often find wriggling worms.

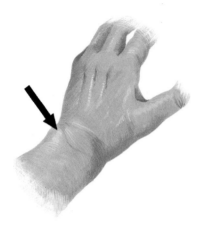

wrist

Your wrist is the part of your body where your hand joins your arm. Your wrist lets you move your hand up and down. You wear a watch or a bracelet on your wrist.

a b c d e f g h i j k l m n o p q r s t u v w x y z

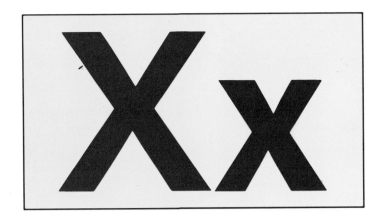

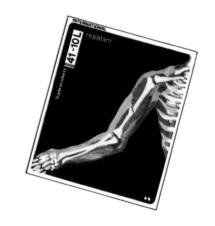

x-ray

An x-ray is a special kind of photograph which lets a doctor see inside your body.

When Ellen fell off the swing she went to the hospital for an x-ray to see if her arm was broken.

xylophone

A xylophone is a musical instrument. You make sounds by hitting flat bars with two hammers.

130

Yy

yacht

A yacht is a small ship with sails.

We watched the yacht at the seaside; its sails looked beautiful in the sunshine.

yellow

Yellow is a colour. Buttercups are yellow and so is the yolk of an egg.

a
b
c
d
e
f
g
h
i
j
k
l
m
n
o
p
q
r
s
t
u
v
w
x
y
z

a
b
c
d
e
f
g
h
i
j
k
l
m
n
o
p
q
r
s
t
u
v
w
x
y
z

Zz

zebra

A zebra is a wild animal which looks like a horse with stripes.

0

zero

Zero means nothing.

zig zag

A zig zag is a pattern which goes up and down. It looks like the letter Z on its side.

zip

A zip is something which joins two pieces of material together. You find zips in clothes.

My jeans fasten with a zip.

zoo

A zoo is a place where you go to see wild animals. In most zoos the animals are kept in cages.

a
b
c
d
e
f
g
h
i
j
k
l
m
n
o
p
q
r
s
t
u
v
w
x
y
z

List of Words

A

acorn	1
acrobat	1
add	1
aerial	2
aeroplane	2
alligator	2
alphabet	2
anchor	2
animal	3
ankle	3
apple	3
apron	3
aquarium	3
arm	4
arrow	4
astronaut	4
athlete	4
axe	4

B

baby	5
back	5
badger	5
bag	5
bagpipes	6
baker	6
ball	6
balloon	6
banana	6
band	7
bandage	7
bank	7
barrel	7
basket	7
bat	8
bath	8

bear	8
bed	8
bee	8
beetle	9
bell	9
bicycle	9
binoculars	9
biscuit	9
bite	10
black	10
blackberry	10
blackboard	10
bleed	10
blow	11
blue	11
boat	11
bone	11
book	11
boot	12
bottle	12
bow	12
box	12
boxer	12
bracelet	13
bread	13
breakfast	13
breathe	13
brick	13
bride	14
bridegroom	14
bridge	14
brown	14
brush	14
bucket	15
bud	15
bulldozer	15
burglar	15
bus	16
butcher	16
butterfly	16
button	16

C

cactus	17
cage	17
cake	17
calculator	17
calf	18
camel	18
camera	18
canary	18
candle	18
canoe	19
cap	19
car	19
caravan	19
carpet	19
carrot	20
carry	20
carve	20
case	20
castle	20
cat	21
catch	21
caterpillar	21
cauliflower	21
cello	21
centipede	22
chain	22
cheer	22
chopsticks	22
church	22
circle	23
city	23
clarinet	23
claw	23
cliff	23
cloak	24
clock	24
cloud	24
clown	24
coat	24